and other Bible Stories

Retold by Vic Parker

Miles
KeLLy

First published in 2011 by Miles Kelly Publishing Ltd
Harding's Barn, Bardfield End Green, Thaxted, Essex, CM6 3PX, UK

2 4 6 8 10 9 7 5 3 1

EDITORIAL DIRECTOR *Belinda Gallagher*
ART DIRECTOR *Jo Cowan*
EDITOR *Carly Blake*
DESIGNERS *Michelle Cannatella, Joe Jones*
JUNIOR DESIGNER *Kayleigh Allen*
COVER DESIGNER *Joe Jones*
CONSULTANT *Janet Dyson*
PRODUCTION MANAGER *Elizabeth Collins*
REPROGRAPHICS *Stephan Davis, Ian Paulyn*

ISBN 978-1-84810-398-6

Printed in China

British Library Cataloguing-in-Publication Data
A catalogue record for this book is available from the British Library

ACKNOWLEDGEMENTS
The publishers would like to thank the following artists
who have contributed to this book:

The Bright Agency Katriona Chapman,
Dan Crisp, Giuliano Ferri (inc. cover)

Advocate Art Andy Catling, Alida Massari

The publishers would like to thank Robert Willoughby and
the London School of Theology for their help in compiling this book.

Made with paper from a sustainable forest

www.mileskelly.net info@mileskelly.net

www.factsforprojects.com

Self-publish your
children's book

buddingpress.co.uk

Contents

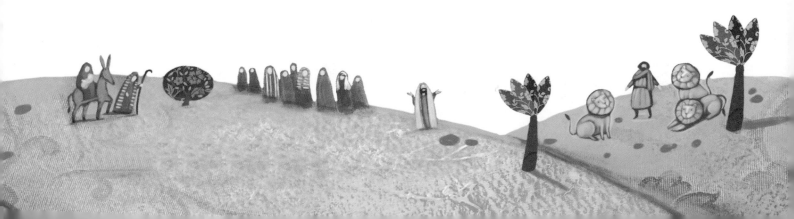

Elijah, Man of God

In the days of King Solomon, one way that eastern kings showed their greatness was to have lots of wives. Solomon had one thousand! Most came from abroad, the marriages arranged to seal peace or trade agreements with other rulers. When Solomon married these foreign women, he let them keep the customs of their country,

including worshipping strange idols. Many of the wives talked Solomon into worshipping them too. God was so furious at this that He punished Solomon by splitting up the nation of Israel.

When Solomon died, only two of the twelve tribes of Israel asked his son to be their king, and his nation came to be known as Judah. The other ten tribes wanted one of Solomon's advisors to rule them instead – they kept the name of Israel for their nation. Both kings turned out to be bad. They, and many of the kings who came after, forgot to be faithful to God at all. God had to seek out good people to speak for Him, to remind everyone what was right and wrong. The people He chose were called prophets, and one very important one was a man called Elijah.

Elijah lived in Israel when a wicked king called Ahab was on the throne, with his even more wicked queen, Jezebel. They both worshipped the idol Baal and of course the people followed them. God sent Elijah to tell the king how he was going to be punished. "God says there will be no rain or dew in your kingdom for three years," Elijah announced, then he fled from Ahab's fury and hid for the duration of the drought.

God worked miracles to keep Elijah alive as the food ran out and water dried up all over Israel. He even gave Elijah the power to work miracles of his own, such as bringing a dead child back to life.

After three years, God told Elijah to meet

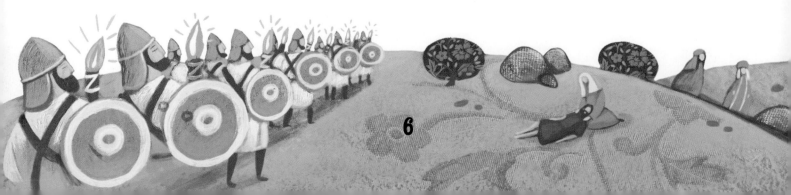

King Ahab on the top of Mount Carmel. Elijah told the king to bring the four hundred and fifty prophets of Baal and the four hundred prophets of the false goddess Asherah. "Now let's see who is real and who isn't – Baal and Asherah, or God," Elijah challenged. "Tell your prophets to build an altar and offer a bull as sacrifice to Baal. I'll do the same. Then let us pray for flames to light the sacrificial fire and see who is answered."

And so the king's prophets built an enormous altar and killed a bull. Then they began dancing and singing around it, calling for Baal to light the fire. All afternoon they went on, but nothing happened.

"You might have to sing louder and

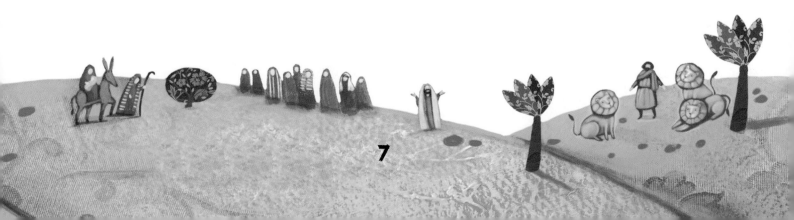

dance harder than that," Elijah laughed. "Perhaps Baal is busy with other things, or maybe he's gone on a trip, or perhaps he's asleep?"

Then Elijah got on with building a little altar to God for his bull. He used a bundle of firewood and twelve stones (to represent the tribes of God's Chosen People). He drenched everything with water until it was completely soaked and filled the trench he had dug around it. Then he stood and said a quiet prayer – a still, lone figure compared to the hundreds of excited, chanting prophets of Baal.

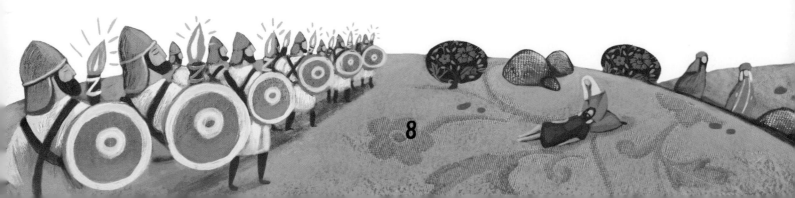

Instantly, fire blazed from Heaven and burned up not just Elijah's bull, but also the wood, the stones, the earth around about – everything. Even the trench full of water hissed and sizzled, and vanished into steam.

The watching crowds fell to the ground in terror.

Then Elijah told Ahab that all the prophets of Baal and Asherah should be put to death, and no one should ever worship idols again. "By the way," Elijah added casually, "you should get a move on if you don't want to get drenched on your way home." For the skies suddenly darkened with black thunder clouds as God prepared to send Israel rain at last.

God stayed with Elijah for the rest of his life and looked after him. Over the years

He spoke many prophecies through him that all came true. God also told Elijah to travel to Syria and find a man called Elisha, whom God wanted as another important prophet. Elijah did so, and Elisha became his constant companion. Elisha was so loyal that he never left his master Elijah's side, even when the time came that the old man knew he was to die. At that moment, a chariot of fire drawn by

blazing horses came thundering towards the two men, forcing them apart. Elisha saw Elijah swept up into the chariot and off into the sky as if by a mighty whirlwind. It circled higher and higher until it became a tiny speck and finally disappeared from view.

And so Elijah was gone, leaving behind only his cloak,

lying on the ground. Elisha picked it up and walked down to the nearby River Jordan. He lashed the river with the cloak and cried out, "Where is the God of Elijah?" To his astonishment, the waters drew back and parted before him. Then Elisha knew that God was with him as He had been with Elijah, and it was up to him to carry on where Elijah had left off.

I Kings chapters 11, 12, 14 to 19; II Kings chapter 2

Elisha and the Leper General

Elisha the holy man travelled around Israel, speaking prophecies for God and working miracles. God gave him so much power that Elisha even once brought a dead child back to life, just as his former master, the prophet Elijah, had done.

News of Elisha's miracles spread far and wide and all sorts of people, rich and poor, begged him for help. One of them was the commander-in-chief of the Syrian army, General Naaman. He suffered from the terrible skin disease, leprosy. He arrived in his smartest uniform, in a huge convoy of gleaming chariots and bodyguards to see Israel's great miracle worker.

This sort of thing didn't impress Elisha. He didn't even bother to come to the door to see the general. He just sent a servant outside with a message: "Wash in the River Jordan seven times and you will be cured."

Well, General Naaman wasn't used to being treated like that. He huffed about in a terrible temper, shouting things like: "The River Jordan is nothing compared to the mighty rivers we have back home in Syria! Why should I wash in a little puddle like that?" It took all Naaman's men to calm him down and convince him to try it.

Six times General Naaman washed himself in the rushing River Jordan. When he emerged after the seventh, his skin was healed.

The overjoyed general hurried back to Elisha and begged him to accept a fortune in silver and gold as a thank you. All the prophet would have was Naaman's promise to worship God from then on.

However, Elisha's servant Gehazi was tempted by the sight of the treasure. When the general set off back to Syria, he galloped after him and lied that Elisha had changed his mind and he would like some money after all. Naaman delightedly sent Gehazi back with as much treasure as a couple of his own servants could carry.

Of course, Elisha mysteriously knew what Gehazi had done. "You have enough money now to buy splendid possessions," he announced to his servant, "but you have also bought Naaman's leprosy too."

In horror, Gehazi looked down to see his hands fester with sores. He stumbled out of Elisha's house with the skin all over his body turning white and dead. Gehazi had been made a leper.

II Kings chapters 4, 5

Jonah and the Whale

One day, God told a man called Jonah, "Go to Assyria, to the capital city of Nineveh. Tell the people there about me and make sure they change their sinful ways."

Jonah didn't care for these people and wasn't much bothered if they found out about God or not. He also didn't like the sound of walking into the capital city of a powerful, war-like nation and telling the people what they were doing wrong. So Jonah got on a boat in the opposite direction to Nineveh, heading for Spain.

As soon as the ship was on its way, God sent a mighty storm. The sailors on baord were terrified and began praying to be saved. Still the rain lashed the boat and the waves hurled it this way and that. Then the sailors decided that someone on board must be cursed. They drew lots and came up with Jonah's name. Shamefully, Jonah

confessed that he was disobeying God by being on the boat. "You'll have to throw me overboard," he wept, "it's the only way this storm will stop." When the storm grew even worse the sailors concluded that they had no choice – and dropped Jonah into the water.

The minute they did so, the wind dropped, the rain stopped and the waves died away. God saved Jonah, too. Instead of letting him drown, He sent a massive fish that swallowed him. For three days Jonah wallowed in the darkness of the fish's belly, praying to God. Finally, the fish spat him out onto a sandy shore.

"Go to Nineveh," God said again, "and give the people my message. If they don't change their behaviour, I will destroy the city after forty days."

This time Jonah did what he was told. To his surprise the Assyrians listened. The king of Nineveh believed God's threat and ordered his people to mend their ways. People started being more polite and kind to each other. They prayed for forgiveness, and started worshipping God, and so God left the city and its people untouched.

Jonah stomped off on his own into the countryside. "I knew this would happen!" he moaned to God, sitting down in protest. "I've come all this way – nearly drowned, been eaten by a fish, faced crowds of hostile strangers – and all for nothing. You haven't

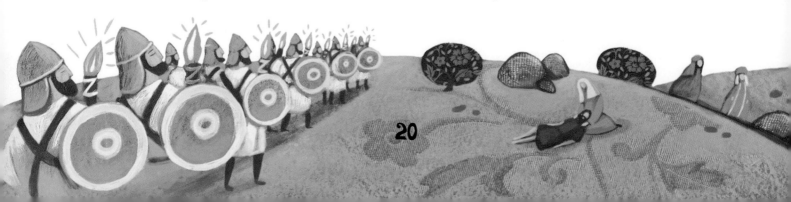

20

punished anyone or destroyed anything."

God decided to teach him a lesson. He made a tree shoot up where Jonah was sitting, so all day he could rest in its shade. But the next day, God sent insects to eat the tree, leaving Jonah sitting in the blazing sun. God also sent desert wind to roast him. "If only my tree hadn't died!" Jonah groaned.

"Well," said God, "if you're upset about a tree – a tree that you neither planted nor looked after – how upset do you think I would have been if Nineveh had been lost? One hundred and twenty thousand people live there, not to mention all the animals."

And Jonah finally understood that God cared for all people, not just the Israelites – and for animals too.

Jonah

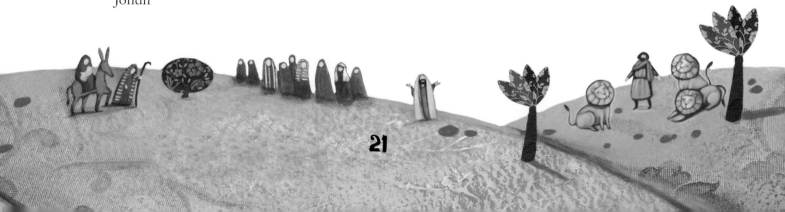

Jeremiah and the End of the Nation

Centuries passed and numerous kings came and went on the thrones of Israel and Judah, who had to fight many enemies.

There came a time when the mighty Assyrians rose up against Israel and Judah. The two nations kept the Assyrian empire at bay by paying an enormous amount of treasure each year. However, the emperor eventually sent his armies to attack Israel. God did not stop them because the Israelites had become too sinful to deserve His help. So the Assyrians crushed the ten tribes of God's Chosen People and took them away in their thousands, back to Assyria to be slaves. They filled Israel's capital city of Samaria with captives brought from other lands they had conquered. These settlers became known as Samaritans.

Around one hundred years went by and God chose a young man called Jeremiah to be His prophet in Judah. "You must warn everyone that unless they change their wicked ways, I will send disaster upon them from the north," God told Jeremiah. God meant that Judah would be overcome by another enemy – the Babylonians, who had become even mightier than the Assyrians. God sent Jeremiah to the house of a potter to watch him shaping clay on his wheel. "Judah is like clay in my hands," God explained to Jeremiah. "If the people do evil, I will crush them. But if they do well, I shall mould them into something good and strong."

Jeremiah told the leaders and people of Judah many times that it was not too late for them to mend their ways. However, they did not listen and God made up his mind that Judah would fall. Jeremiah told the people this and he even

took to wearing a yoke, a harness for an ox, around his neck as a sign to everyone that they would soon be made slaves.

The Judeans hated Jeremiah for his prophecies of destruction, but of course they came true. Nebuchadnezzar, king of Babylon, sent a huge army to attack Judah. The city of Jerusalem was seized and most of the people were taken back to Babylon in chains.

"Do not fear," God told Jeremiah, "when my people in exile repent for their sins, I will bring them out of captivity and restore the kingdom of Israel as a united, great nation once more."

II Kings chapters 17, 18, 25; Jeremiah chapters 1, 18, 24, 27, 31, 39

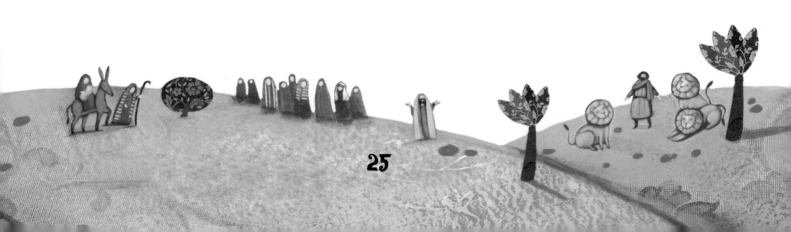

Nebuchadnezzar's Dream

King Nebuchadnezzar, Emperor of Babylon, was very clever. When he conquered other countries and took their peoples captive, he got his officials to look for those who had special talents so he could put them to good use for himself.

Daniel and his three friends Shadrach, Meshach and Abednego were among a few young captive Israelite men selected to be trained as advisors to the king. They worked hard and God gave them extra skills as a reward. God made Daniel very good at telling the meaning of dreams and visions.

One morning, the king called an emergency meeting of his advisors. "I have had a worrying dream," Nebuchadnezzar announced, "and I want someone to explain to me what it means."

"Tell us the dream, Your Majesty, and we'll be glad to interpret what it means," replied his advisors, bowing low.

"No," announced Nebuchadnezzar, with a glint in his steely eyes. "You could make up any meaning you like. I want someone to tell me both the dream and the meaning. Only then will I be convinced of the truth."

"And by the way," he added coldly, "if no one can do it, I'll have every one of you put to death."

Daniel begged the king for time, and he, Shadrach, Meshach and Abednego asked God for help. And so God sent Daniel a dream, which told him everything.

"You saw a massive statue," Daniel told Nebuchadnezzar. "Its head was gold, its chest and arms silver, its belly and thighs bronze, its legs iron and its feet half iron and half clay. Then an enormous stone bashed against the statue's feet and the statue toppled and smashed into dust. Then the stone grew into a mountain that covered all the earth.

"This dream means that your empire is like the head of gold, greatest of all. The silver, bronze and iron are three kingdoms that will come after yours, each less powerful than the one before. The last kingdom will be divided into two and will be partly strong and partly weak. But no empire will last until God's kingdom comes and replaces all others forever."

Nebuchadnezzar was astonished and delighted. "Your god must indeed be the god of all gods," he marvelled. He rewarded Daniel and made him chief of his wise men.

Daniel chapters 1, 2

Daniel in the Lions' Den

When Nebuchadnezzar died, Belshazzar became the new king of Babylon. After him, King Darius of the Medes and Persians seized the throne.

Daniel was such an outstanding advisor that King Darius put him in charge of his whole empire. The other officials were so jealous that they came up with an idea that would land Daniel in trouble. They suggested to Darius that he should order that no one should pray to anyone but him for thirty days. If anyone disobeyed, they were to be thrown into a pit of lions. The king thought it was a great idea and signed the order.

Now Daniel was a good, holy man. Of course, he continued to pray to God three times a day, as always in front of his window in full view of passers-by.

It wasn't long before his enemies reported him to the king. Darius was devastated, but he could not go back on his word. He ordered that Daniel should be thrown into the den of lions. "May your god save you," the king prayed, and a huge stone was placed over the pit so there was no way Daniel could escape.

Darius spent all night thinking about how he had caused Daniel to be flung to the lions. As soon as dawn came he hurried to the pit and yelled out, "Daniel! Was God with you? Are you still alive?"

To Darius' relief, Daniel answered, "Yes, sire. God sent an angel to guard me and the lions have left me untouched."

The king ordered that Daniel be pulled out of the pit and all the wicked people who had accused him thrown in instead.

The lions tore them to bits until nothing but bones were left.

Daniel chapter 6

Queen Esther the Brave

King Xerxes was a mighty Persian king whose empire stretched from India to Ethiopia. He was once so displeased with his wife, Vashti, that he announced she was no longer his queen. He ordered for beautiful young women to be brought from all corners of his empire to the palace so he could choose a new wife.

One of the men who worked in the royal household was an old Jew called Mordecai. He urged his adopted daughter Esther to go to the palace and take part in the beauty competition. Mordecai warned her not to tell anyone she was his daughter or that she was Jewish, for many people hated the captives who had been brought from Israel.

Esther did as she was told and went to the palace. For a year she was pampered with beauty treatments, and had lessons in grooming and how to behave like a queen. When all the candidates were presented to the king, Xerxes chose Esther as his queen. He soon found that she wasn't just a pretty face either. He came to like her very much.

One day, Esther told the king how Mordecai had overheard two servants

plotting to kill him, and Xerxes believed Esther at once. He had the two men arrested and hanged, and ordered for the event to be written down in his official Book of Records. Mordecai and Esther had saved his life.

Some time later, King Xerxes made a man called Haman his chief minister and the king commanded his subjects to bow before him. Mordecai always refused. "I bow to none other than God," the old man would insist. This disobedience drove Haman quite mad. He was determined to have revenge. Not just on Mordecai, but on all Jewish people. He told the king that the Jews were disobedient and nothing but trouble, and that his kingdom would be better off if he had them all put to death.

"Whatever you think best," Xerxes told his trusted minister, and gave Haman his royal seal to sign the execution warrant.

When Mordecai found out he was appalled, and begged Esther to ask Xerxes for mercy. She dressed in her finest robes and went unsummoned into the king's presence, an action for which the law said she could have been put to death. Luckily, the king was happy to see her and said she could have whatever she had come for.

"All I would like is for you and Haman to be my guests at dinner tomorrow," Esther said charmingly, and King Xerxes agreed.

Esther held a wonderful dinner for the men, with delicious food and wity conversation in beautiful surroundings.

Having begun to win her husband and his minister over, she invited them to another dinner the following night, when she hoped she could finish the job and ask for forgiveness for the Jews. Little did she know that later that very evening Haman had ordered that a gallows

be built at the palace. They were to hang the man he hated – Mordecai, her father. At around the same time, Xerxes was being read aloud to from the Book of Records. The reader happened to announce the entry that described how Mordecai had helped foil the earlier plot to kill King Xerxes and it reminded the king that he had never honoured the man.

Just then, a servant announced that Haman was asking to see him. He hadcome to ask for the king's permission to execute Mordecai.

"Now Haman, tell me what you would do to reward a man you wanted to

honour," wondered the king, as his chief minister was ushered in.

Haman tried to hide a smug smirk. He thought that he must be the man the king wanted to honour. "Such a person should be dressed in robes fit for a king and paraded on one of your own horses through the streets as a hero," Haman sighed.

"What a good idea!" Xerxes said, delighted. "Then that's what I want you to do for Mordecai the Jew in the morning."

Haman was outraged. By the time he arrived at the queen's second supper, his face was sulky and ugly.

This time, Esther begged Xerxes for mercy. She confessed that she was a Jew and that orders had been given for all Jewish people to be put to death.

"Who has dared to do such a terrible thing?" boomed the king, outraged.

"The man who is sitting beside you," Esther said quietly. "Haman."

Choked with fury, Xerxes strode out into the palace gardens. He returned to find Haman at Esther's feet, begging for mercy, but it looked as though he was attacking her. To make matters worse, one of Esther's servants told the king that Haman had built a gallows to kill Mordecai.

The king did not delay in having Haman executed. Then he sent letters throughout his empire, ordering that the Jews should be respected.

And that is how the brave, beautiful Esther saved her people, the Israelites.

Esther chapters 1 to 8